Cricut for begginers 2021

Learn How To Use Your Cricut Machine And Cricut Space Design With Step-By-Step Guide To Get Everything Up And Running In No Time

ANGELA BAKER

Table of contents

Introduction

The invention of the Cricut device certainly transformed the booking & removing sport of craft. With its rotational cutter, this new tool can cut detailed symbols and patterns from various printing methods as well as provide a tailored, efficient, and quick, easy-to-make touch. With paper, contemporary Cricut could still do incredible stuff, although they are capable of doing much more. The combination of the machine and the tools of the crunch model allows you greater artistic flexibility than it has ever been, and that you can choose a wide variety of materials for your Cricut with a huge assortment of tool attachments. This device is important for its simplicity and efficiency of use for both artisans and lovers.

Chapter 1: Cricut Machine

1.1 What Is a Cricut Machine?

Cricut is a brand name of a computer device that cuts a range of products, including paper, hard card, and vinyl stickers, and, in case you have an advanced version, you may cut fabrics. It works through an online software, that is known as Design Space. Using this, you can purchase, upload, or build your plans, and this device can cut it for its owners. It also holds a good feature called "Print and Cut" that helps you print your template on a standard home printer and then put it into the Cricut device to be cut according to size. Additionally, for cutting, you may also buy extra tools that enable your device to compose fancy calligraphy, perforate beautiful lines or engrave intricate designs.

In reality, if you wish to use Cricut as a printer, the good news is you can do that as well! There is a dedicated accessory slot available in your machine

1. Create Your Design

To create a design, you can use the Cricut Design Space free application for your Computer or Mac Operating System. You can use the Design Space application for the iOS operating system while using your iPhone or iPad device, or the beta edition of the Design Space application for Android is easily available. Design Space is a software that links your computer system to your Cricut device. Cricut Design Space application library is filled with thousands of pre-made templates available to be imported and rebuild by yourself.

You can create the project the same as you have planned it or modify it if you want. When you select a Design Space Library project, you'll see choices to modify it (then you can adjust it, optimize text, etc.); further, you can build a brand-new concept from Scrape inside Design Space utilizing their designing software. You can edit text, pictures, upload your photos, resize, change the design, etc., to build an ideal design.

When your project looks as you wish it to be, that's the time to prepare the Cricut device.

3. Transfer the Design to Your Machine

The final move is to submit the task to the Cricut device. Once you're satisfied with your model and your device is turned on, click the wide green-colored "MAKE IT" button at the upper right side of the Cricut Design Area.

The software begins with an overview of your various mats. Every mat is a single sheet of paper, and in that case, where you have three multiple colors for your project, you have three multiple mats. If you are using paper and cloth for a design, then you will also have a single mat for each material.

Chapter 2: Introduction to Infusible Ink and DIY Projects

Circuit's sublimation edition is Infusible Paint, and it's awesome! There are two methods of using Infusible Ink at the moment this book is being written.

Infusible Ink Pens: use these pens to draw either manually or by using the pen extension on your Cricut on projector copy paper. First, use heating to incorporate one of Circuit's Infusible Ink blanks with the template.

Infusible Ink Shift Sheets: imagine as you would iron-on for Infusible Ink Transfer Sheets. In the Infusible Ink Transfer Sheet, use your Cricut to cut a layout, grow your project, and use heat to incorporate the design into Circuit's Infusible Ink Blanks directly.

Available: Cricut Infusible Ink Blanks

- ✓ Tote bags

- ✓ Coasters

- ✓ Shirts

- ✓ Onesies

2.1 Could We Use Our Blanks of Infusible Ink?

This is one of Infusible Ink's most popular issues. Are you able to? Sure! Oh, yes! Do you have to? That's another issue. In producing Infusible Ink, Cricut expended a great deal of time and science. Any time you use them, the tops, onesies, coasters, and totes are all made of fabrics that have been specially created to give you the best, longest-lasting performance. Infusible Ink is not soaked into normal blank tiles. You will be able to infuse Infusible Ink onto other blanks of fabric; however, most people have indicated that the color is not as vivid, and the design's longevity is not very good.

2.2 How Does Infusible Ink Vary From Iron-on?

In certain ways, Infusible Ink Transfer Sheets and Iron-on are very related. You pick a pattern for both, mirror the design, lay the sheet's color side down on the cutting pad, clip, plant, and use heat to move. Your ended product is the ultimate difference. The Infusible Ink is infused into the blank indefinitely. That becomes one with the stuff you have! Since the blank is infused into it, that means it's flawless! It will feel flat as you rub your hand over your blank one. Through touch, there's no distinction from where the Ink is diluted where it's not. There's no fingerprint smudges, no flaking skin, no splitting, and no dimpling as the Infusible Ink becomes one with the blank! It's truly like sorcery.

2.3 Infusible Ink Succulent Coasters

For this venture, we wanted to draw a series of succulents for you that you could turn through your own coasters.

Machine: Cricut Explore or Cricut Maker Project (Cricut Joy Compatible)

Items:

- Lint roller

- Cricut Heat Resistant Tape

- Butcher paper

- Fine-tip blade

- Cricut Easy Press 2

- Cricut Easy Press Mat

- Cardstock

- LightGrip cutting mat

- Infusible Ink blank coasters

- Succulent drawing files

- Infusible Ink pens

- Laser copy paper

Directions:

Phase 1: sign in to the Cricut Design Space and construct four circles, every 3.5 inches wide, using the Shape tool. Submit a design file for Succulent.

Phase 2: scale the succulents to 3.25 inches by 3.25 inches and adjust to create the line type.

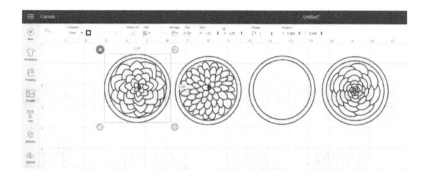

Phase 3: focus on the top of one of the rings for one succulent illustration. Hit Attach to guarantee that perhaps the succulent and circle are both picked. For the four succulents, do that now.

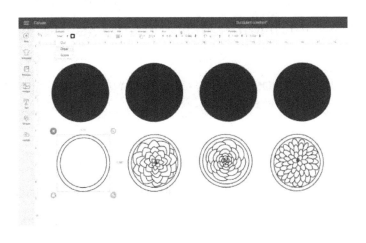

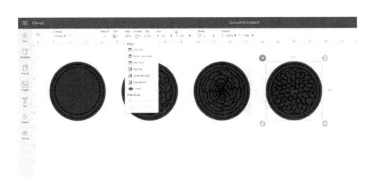

Phase 4: please press Make It. Adjust the dimension of the product to 8.5 x 11 inches. To reflect your portrait, move the mirror slider.

Move 5: as your cutting material, use Laser Copy Paper. Press the cute little Cricut C on your device to begin cutting! Mount your Infusible Ink Pen into your system, place a sheet of laser copy paper on your slicing mat and launch it into your device. Just sit back and watch the sketch for Cricut.

Phase 6: take the succulent circles off the cutting board kindly. For coloring them in, utilize your Infusible Ink Pens.

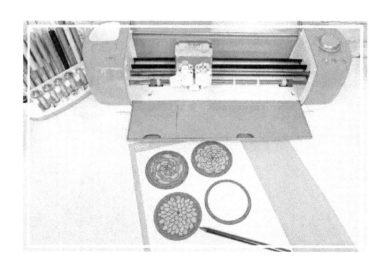

Phase 7: set the heat to 400 °F for your Cricut Easy Press 2 and 240 seconds for your timer. Layout and cover your Easy Press Mat with a piece of cardstock.

With the shiny side looking ahead, place your coaster on your Easy Press Mat. To clean any mud or gunk from your coaster, use a gunk roller or a lint-free rag. It's a crucial step to ensure that the design imbues the coaster correctly. Do not miss this process.

With the painted side facing down, place your pattern on your coaster. To place the pattern into place, use your Cricut Heat Resistance Tape.

Switch the coaster so that the pattern faces down, covering the coaster with butcher paper, and use your Cricut Easy Press 2 to press. Do not jump about on Easy Press. With firm, constant pressure, holding it as still as possible.

Gently raise your Easy Press, being cautious not to stop the coaster, as your Easy Press buzzes that perhaps the timer is over. It's supposed to be really hot on your roller, so don't handle it. Once your coaster is cooler, leaving well enough alone.

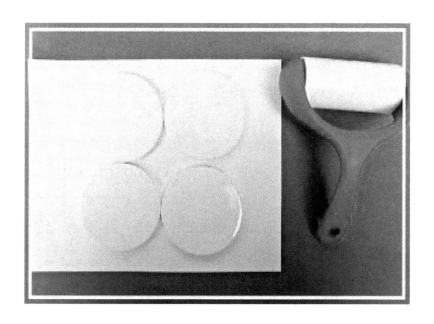

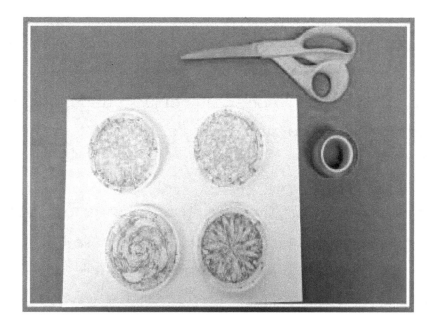

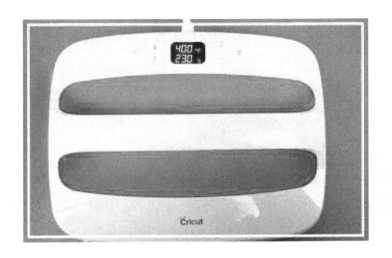

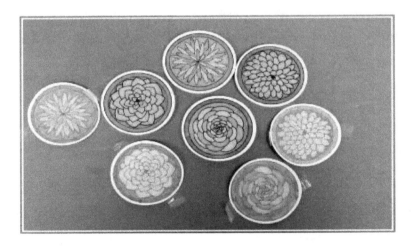

For these coasters, the options are still infinite. You can draw whatever you want to move onto the coasters, as far as you have Infusible Ink Pens & laser copy paper. You could also cut patterns to be mounted on coasters out of Cricut Infusible Ink Transfer Cards.

2.4 Homegrown Onesie

Let's be blunt. Place children's clothing into the wringer! On toddler clothing, from spit up, baby formula, and blowouts on onesies to PB&J smears, lawn streaks, and mud pie splatters. You just don't know how much time sucking laundry will take before you become a mom. After a couple of washes, HTV will ultimately strip, and that was one of the reasons we love Infusible Ink for kids' clothes! Since Infusible Ink absorbs straight into the apparel, there is no chance of the pattern scraping after a hundred and one rinses. We use a basic pattern for this "Homegrown" Infusible Ink onesie, and then let the Infusible Ink Transfer Sheet super glow! So we figured that it was great to make an onesie said that "homegrown" in a gorgeous floral pattern. Cricut offers many awesome Infusible Ink Transfer Sheets designs, so making sure you start it all out and see how your artistic creativity takes you! Also, do not even overlook how you can produce shirts like the Monster Family Portrait project using the Infusible Ink pen.

Machine: Cricut Explore or Cricut Maker Project (Cricut Joy Compatible)

Items:

- Lint roller

- Cricut Easy Press 2

- Optional: Brayer tool and heat-safe tape

- Butcher paper

- Measuring tape

- Regular grip cutting mat

- Infusible Ink baby onesie

- Homegrown cut file

- Cricut floral Infusible Ink transfer sheet from Shaylee collection

- Weeding tools

- Fine-tip blade

- Cricut Easy Press Mat

- Cardstock

Directions:

Phase 1: use the Cut File Upload guidelines to sign into Cricut Design Space and import the Homegrown cut file.

Phase 2: in order to decide how large you want the concept to be, weigh your own. By clicking on the interface or using whether the arrow sizer in the corner or the Sizing tool in the upper toolbar, size your version accordingly.

Phase 3: please press Make It. Slide on the cutting mat with the mirror slider. Lie the Infusible Ink Transfer Layer on the cutting pad with the paint facing up and the filler facing down. We want to roll a brayer over the top of our transfer sheet to ensure that it's always pressed down on the cutting mat and won't slip when cutting. Choose your slicing stuff, use the arrow button to load your slicing mat into your printer, and then to start cutting, press the sweet little Cricut C on your machine! Click the arrow again when your computer is finished cutting to offload the mat.

Phase 4: weed the sample, cut the extra transfer sheet from about your layout, keeping the transparent plastic backing with only your design. The field from around the heart, and afterwards each of the letters would be withdrawn, retaining the letter centers in place.

Notice that the substance of the transfer layer is thinner than it is until pressed.

Phase 5: heat up to 385 °F with your Cricut Easy Press. Place your onesie on top of your Cricut Easy Press Pad, and then place a piece of cardstock within your onesie to avoid leakage via the back of the Infusible Ink. Use your gunk roller to clear your onesies from any dog hair or dust spores.

On the highest point of your onesie, lay a butcher paper sheet and heat it for 15 seconds. At this stage, do not skip it. Heating the onesie eliminates all humidity from the cloth, helps the Infusible Ink incorporate the fabric correctly, and acts like magic!

Drop the butcher paper and lay your pattern on your onesie in which you would like it. Place your butcher papers back at the top of the onesie and afterward click for 40 seconds with your Easy Press. Use relentless pressure and be cautious not to slip or move your hands across the Easy Press when it is being squeezed. You want your Easy Press to stay under firm pressure at all times. Raise the Easy Press carefully at the end of 40 seconds and leave your onesie to cool with the butcher paper on top of the pattern.

Remove the butcher paper until your design has settled, and gently peel up a plastic liner, exposing your design!

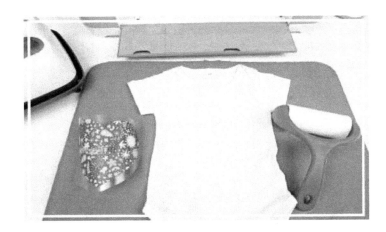

Note: use a pair of pliers to push it up gently if the transition layer does not really come with a plastic backing.

Clean the unit inside out with a gentle cleanser with ice water. Low dry tumble or dry line tumble. Should not use softener, dryer sheets, or chlorine for clothing.

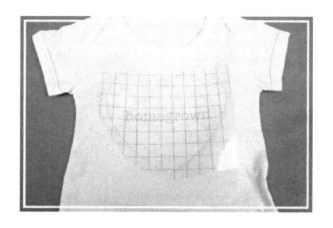

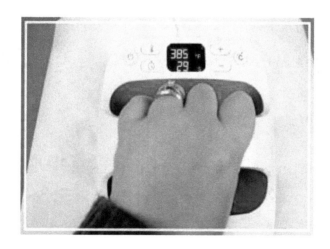

This adorable little onesie is a super cute present for a baby shower; making a whole collection of various designs of transition sheets and styles of Infusible Ink onesies!

2.5 Drink and Food Coaster

Let us just finish our ride through Infusible Ink with coaster design! We utilized Circuit's circular ceramic Infusible Ink Coasters for our succulent coasters paired with Infusible Ink pens. We will use Circuit's cork-backed Infusible Ink square coasters coupled with Infusible Ink Rainbow Transfer Sheets in this venture. Have you got an idea about somebody else saying you'd love to have a coaster? At Cricut Design Space, create your first! With a Cricut Access membership, the Kyden font is accessible and very close to the font we included in this project.

Machine: Cricut Explore or Cricut Maker Project (Cricut Joy Compatible)

Items:

- Cricut Rainbow Infusible Ink Transfer Sheet

- Cricut Easy Press Mat

- Cardstock

- Lint roller or lint-free cloth

- Butcher paper

- Cricut Easy Press 2

- Food & Drink Coaster cut files

- Infusible Ink cork-backed square coaster blanks

- Regular grip cutting mat

- Fine-tip blade

Phase 1: sign in and import the Food & Drink Cut File to the Cricut Design Space.

Phase 2: by clicking on each coaster template and using whether another arrow sizer in the corner of the Scale boxes in the upper toolbar, size each coaster file to 4 x 4 inches. (The square coasters of Cricut measure 3.75 x 3.75 inches. Sizing the models 4 x4 inches can allow any border across each coaster so that you really can ensure it is fully coated with infusible Ink.)

Phase 3: please press Make It. Slide on the cutting mat with the mirror slider. Place your coasters on your cutting mat where you'd like them. In order to have various rainbow color combos on each coaster, we decided to spread our coasters around the transfer board. Lay the Infusible Ink transfer layer on the cutting mat with the painted face up and the lining facing down. We would like to roll a brayer over the edge of our transfer sheet to ensure that it's always pressed down on the cutting mat and won't slip when cutting. Select your cutting stuff, use the arrow button to mount your cutting mat into your device, and then to start to cut, press the pretty little Cricut C on your device! Click the arrow once more when your device is finished cutting; to offload the mat.

Weed the coaster patterns, scraping from around each coaster the Infusible Ink and the letters from inside. Be sure to leave the letter centers, like the a, p, r, and so on. Break around each coaster so that on a piece of the plastic backing, it is by itself.

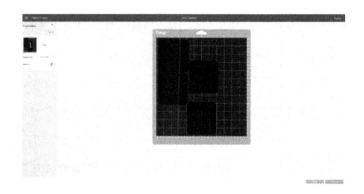

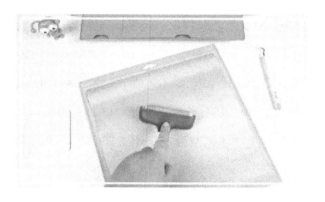

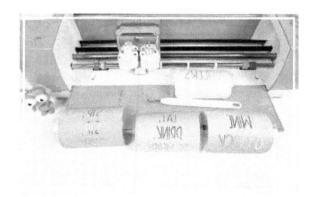

Phase 4: set the temperature to 400 °F for your Cricut Easy Press 2 and 240 seconds for your timer. Spread out and cover your Easy Press Pad with a piece of cardstock.

With the glossy side facing up, place your coaster on your Easy Press Mat. To clean any mud or lint from your coaster, use a lint roller or a glitch rag. Do not miss this step; making sure your concept imbues the coaster appropriately is a significant one.

With the color side facing up, lay the pattern on the cardstock. With the white side facing downward, put your coaster on top of the pattern. Cover with a butcher's sheet of paper. Click with your Easy Press 2 Cricut. Do not jump about on Easy Press. Keeping it as calm as possible and put constant, strong pressure.

If your Easy Press buzzes that now the timer is over, raise your Easy Press slowly, making sure the coaster is not disturbed. It's going to be really hot on your roller, so don't touch it. Leave until your coaster is cold to the touch to encourage your Ink to stop blending. Lift it up until the coaster is cold, removing the coaster from the build.

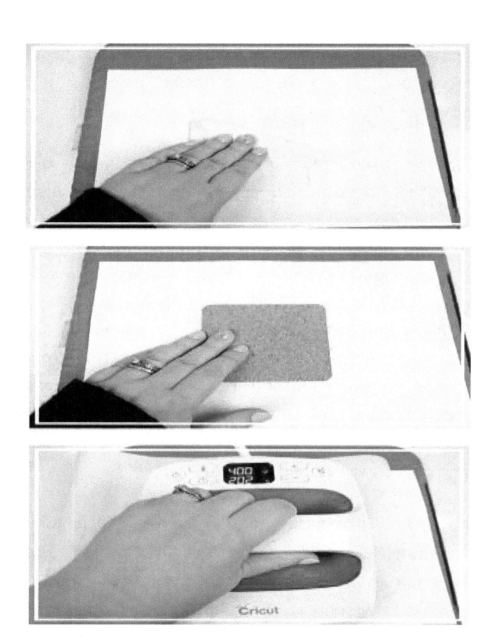

And you've got it there! The Infusible Ink Coasters are just so much joy indeed! They make perfect housewarming gifts, and the options are indeed infinite between the use of Infusible Ink Transfer Sheets and Infusible Ink pens!

Chapter 3: DIY Basswood, Balsa Wood, and Chipboard Projects

The Cricut Knife Blade unlocked the way to an entirely new universe of craft potential, particularly for home decor crafters! By cutting plasterboard, Basswood, & Balsa Wood, you may create so many wonderful things.

We're not sugarcoating it: it takes patience for your Cricut Maker to cut Basswood, balsa wood, including chipboard. There's a bit of an adjustment to it, and when you're struggling to pull them off the pad, or even when you feel irritated that the knife blade just doesn't cut all the way across, there'll be moments when your creations split. Yeah, it can be a challenging process, but it is so awesome when your project turns out exactly the way you imagined it would! We included some knife blade performance tips down, so you're going to be a professional before long!

3.1 Cricut Builder Knife Blade Tips for Success

✓ Firstly, please ensure that the knife blade is calibrated after installing it into the unit. This takes just a second and uses a sheet of paper, certainly worth the time to have the cutting accuracy. Log in to Cricut Design Room to do this. You'll see a rectangle consisting of three lines in the upper left-hand corner. Press the square, and a calibration-listed pop-up menu appears. Press Calibration and the instructions are followed.

✓ Ensure that the template is dimensioned such that no region is smaller than a pencil eraser. It will help prevent the splitting of pieces.

✓ Be sure to switch all 4 of the white star wheels to your device's right-hand side. The white star wheels on the front of the unit can be located on the metal roller rod, which your mat goes under. Pull those bad boys to the right all the way.

✓ Please ensure you have a full width of 11 inches for the cutting material.

✓ In the upper left-hand corner of your mat, place your chipboard, Basswood, or balsa wood. By Utilizing masking tape or painter's tape, tape the cutting material to the pad.

✓ To conclude your idea, make sure you set aside time. The knife blade functions until it slices all the way through the product by making several cuts. This could actually take hours for your device to cut, based on how massive your project is.

✓ Talking of time, you do not want to set up your computer and leave it behind. We strongly recommend that you make sure that every few cuts, you review your work/do not leave your computer unattended. As the computer begins cutting on the Cricut Design Space panel, it will say something like "3 out of 12 cuts completed, 20 minutes remain." If you are using your project with a brand spanking new sharp edge, the knife will cut through much faster than Design Space thinks.

Using the Pause button on the Cricut Maker device, you can verify your job.

✓ Play about with a mirrored cut of the design. By cutting their materials with a mirrored knife blade, some crafters swear and think that they get a cleaner cut on the section nearest to the mat. Experiment with your picture being replicated to see what you think!

✓ As cutting with a knife blade requires very much longer than cutting with other blades, sacrificing your link to your device is the last thing you would want to do! You will want to connect your device to your Cricut Creator directly using a USB cable. When their knife blade is cutting, some of our crafty friends even advise not running other applications on their machines.

3.2 DIY Snap Puzzle

This project is simple to do, but this will take your Cricut about an hour to cut due to the pattern's extreme complexities and slicing it out of the chipboard; please ensure you weigh in patience if you make this as a homemade present. Choose your favorite picture and let the fun start!

Machine: Cricut Maker

Items:

- Masking or painter's tape

- Cricut knife blade

- Glue

- Printer

- LightGrip cutting mat

- Your favorite photo

- Printable vinyl

- Fine-point blade

- Cricut chipboard in either 1.5mm or 2mm

- Strong Grip cutting mat

Directions:

Phase 1: press the Upload button to submit a photo to Cricut Design Space, pick your file, choose Complicated Image, and then save your document as a print-and-cut file.

Phase 2: press the "Image" key and check for "Puzzle." Choose one of the puzzle-cut files for Cricut.

Phase 3: tap on the puzzle's layout and select Ungroup from the menu on the right. In Design Space, place the solid bottom piece of the puzzle on the top of your photo; over the picture where you'd like the puzzle to be, put it at the base of the puzzle. Pick your picture as well as the puzzle part at the bottom and press the Slice button. Your picture is now going to be trimmed to the same scale as your puzzle. Remove the extra chunks.

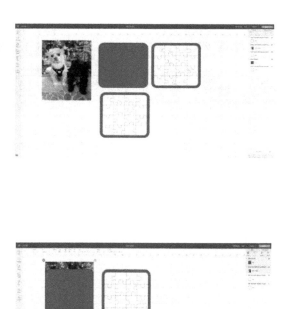

Phase 4: to clone the puzzle's section, which has the puzzle bits, press Duplicate. Position it over your picture at the end. Position the puzzle and the images in order to match up all the edges. Press Attach, with the Lego blocks and the photo all lined up and picked.

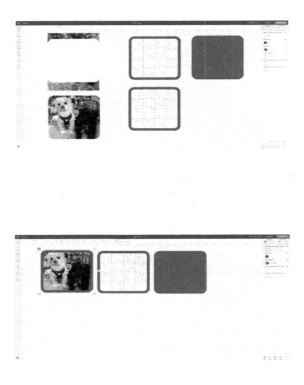

Phase 5: please press Make It. You'll be asked to print your picture first, Do it on your printable vinyl cover. After this, we placed the printed vinyl on a cutting board for the LightGrip, load it into the computer, and cut it. Let the machine cut, then unload the mat.

Phase 6: now, it is time for the chipboard to be removed. Slide your cutting machine's white star wheels to your machine's right-hand side. On a Strong Grip cutting pad, put a piece of chipboard on it. Use masking tape or painter's tape to position the tape in place. Pick your mats, which will be cut out of the chipboard on the left-hand side of the panel. Select the Edit function to shift the cut down to 1 inch and 1 inch to the right. Switch to chipboard with your cutting stuff. Place the knife blade in your Cricut, and then click the arrow and push the blinking Cricut C to mount your cutting mat into the device. Repeat step 6 with the next piece of the puzzle with the second version of the chipboard.

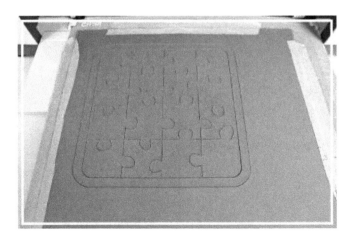

Phase 7: to every piece of the puzzle, pass your vinyl stickers. You can make the boundary out of your printed vinyl picture, or you can paint the chipboard with your favorite color as an option.

Phase 8: on a work-safe board, lay the bottom of your puzzle. Glue the border on top of the bottom of the puzzle. Enable your puzzle to dry and afterward complete it!

Photo puzzles make an outstanding crafted present. For the fiftieth anniversary gift, place an old wedding picture on a puzzle. For a first birthday gift, place a newborn picture on a puzzle. For a one-of-a-kind teacher present, put a class picture on a puzzle! What are you going to put your picture puzzle on?

3.3 LLAMA Pencil Holder

To adorn your llama jar with beautiful adornments, use your creativity! Mess around with the colors you are using for its suspenders, make a beautiful flower crown, or customize it with multicolored yarn on the rim of the jar!

Machine: Cricut Maker

Items:

- Transfer tape

- Strong Grip cutting mat

- Brayer or scraper

- Glue gun and hot glue sticks

- Masking or painter's tape

- Llama cut file

- Mason jar

- Ruler or measuring tape

- Cricut chipboard in either 1.5mm or 2mm

- Cricut Knife Blade

- Vinyl Foam paintbrush

- Acrylic paint

- Weeding tools

- Optional: Extra embellishments to decorate your llama

Phase 1: sign in and upload the Llama pencil holder cut file to Cricut Design Space.

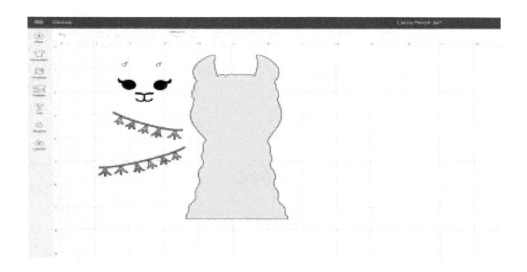

Phase 2: to decide how big you really want your llama to be, weigh your mason jar. We made it 7 inches tall. By tapping on it and either using the arrow, which is in the design's bottom right, or the Sizing feature in the top toolbar, scale the layout.

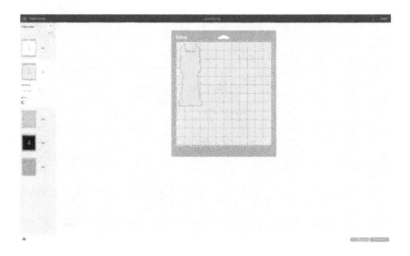

Phase 3: please press Make It. We found that our chipboard cuts smoother on the side nearest to the mat, so press the mirror slider from each mat on the left of the screen; we recommend replicating each of the bits. Use a Strong Grip pad and a knife blade to slice the llama body from the chipboard. To mount the chipboard to the cutting mat, use masking tape or painter's tape.

For carving the eyes, nose, lips, and tassels out of vinyl, use a standard grip mat, including your fine-tip razor.

Using an arrow on the right-hand side of the Cricut to mount your cutting mat into the unit after the cues on the screen. Wait for the Cricut C to begin blinking once your mat is loaded, click the trigger, and your computer will start cutting. Click the arrow again as your computer stops cutting, and it will unload your mat.

Phase 4: color your llama and mason jar with chipboard, enabling the paint to dry for each coat.

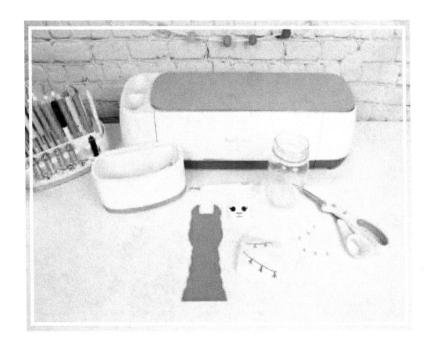

Phase 5: weed the vinyl, strip the region on each design and leave the paper backing with only the design.

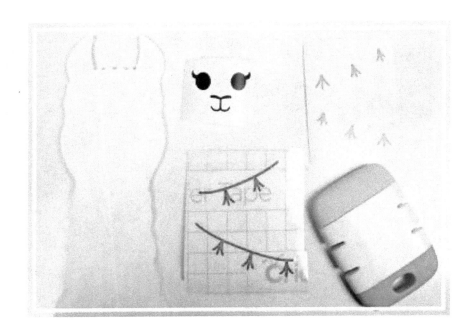

Phase 6: slice a piece of transfer tape a little bit smaller than your biggest vinyl template until the color has settled on your llama. Shave the paperback off the transfer tape and place it so that one of your vinyl designs is sitting on top of the sticky portion. Rub the surface of the transfer tape with your sanding sponge or brayer tool, moving the tape onto the vinyl. Peel the transfer tape and cut the vinyl from the back of the file. Place the transfer tape over your llama where it is appropriate to lay the vinyl pattern. Force down the transfer tape on the llama and pass the brayer or remover tool over the pattern. Shave up the transfer tape gently, placing the pattern on the llama. Repeat for each of the concept bits.

Phase 7: apply some additional adornments to your llama, which you might like, then use your hot glue gun to glue your llama to the mason jar.

With your favorite craft materials and instruments, complete your llama. It makes the small desktop planner the prettiest!

3.4 Star Basswood Wall Décor

In a child's room or used to beautify the space of someone who wants a hint of beauty, which comes through dreaming for stars, this project will look cute!

Machine: Cricut Maker

Items:

- Weeding tools

- Transfer tape (if using vinyl)

- Brayer or scraper

- Vinyl or iron-on in color you would like the star and the word wish

- "Wish Upon a Star" cut file

- Two pieces Cricut basswood, 11 × 11 inches

- Strong Grip cutting mat

- Regular grip cutting mat

- Fine-tip cutting blade

- Masking or painter's tape

- Cricut knife blade

- Glue

- Heavy book

- Cricut Easy Press or iron (if using iron-on)

Directions:

Phase1: sign in to the Cricut Design Space, then import the cut file "Wish Upon a Star."

Phase 2: after tapping on it and either using the arrow, which resides in the lower right-hand corner of the layout, or the Size option in the top toolbar, scale the design such that your star is 10 inches wide. Copy a star so you'll have two of them. To ensure you recall removing this from iron-on or vinyl, adjust your second star's shade. By tapping on it and then hitting a Double icon (we're trying to layer our Basswood, so it's double layers thick after that one layer of iron-on or vinyl), you get three of them. To make you know to remove it from iron-on or vinyl, change the hue of one wish.

Phase 3: please press Make It using the knife blade to sever one of the stars and two wishes from Basswood. Utilizing painter's tape or masking tape, clip the Basswood to the Strong Grip pad.

Out of iron-on or vinyl, slice one star and one wish using a normal grip pad and a blade with a fine-point. Be certain to replicate them by using a mirror slider below each mat on the left of the screen when you're using iron-on for all of the parts. Note that perhaps the color/shiny side of the iron-on goes down on the cutting mat.

Using the arrow on the right-hand side of your Cricut to mount your cutting pad into the unit after the prompts on the monitor. Wait for the Cricut C to begin blinking once your mat is mounted, click the key, and your device will start to cut. Click the arrow again when your machine stops slicing, and it will offload your mat.

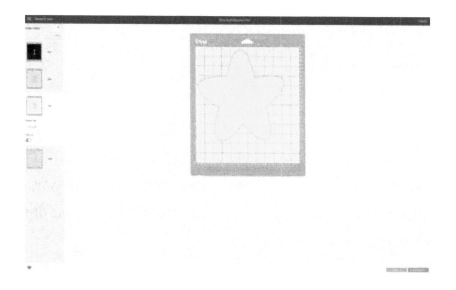

Phase 4: glue each other with your two sets of the word want, so it's two layers deep. To push it together and rinse, put a heavy book on edge.

Phase 5: weed the vinyl or iron-on, eliminating the area surrounding each model, replacing the paper backing with only the design.

Phase 6: add your iron-on or vinyl to your star and wish terms until the glue has dried. If iron-on is used, follow the suggestions for heat temperature to apply the sort of iron-on you are using to wood and using transfer tape when using vinyl to transfer the vinyl to each basswood form.

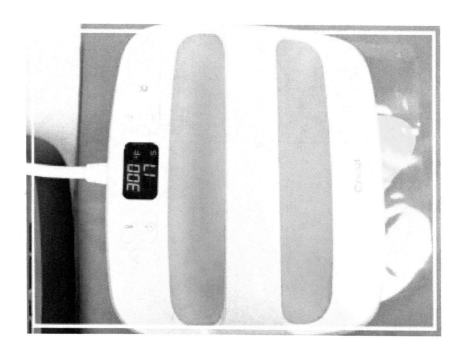

Phase 7: glue the wish to your star in front of you. On top, place a heavy book and allow the glue to dry.

Connect the back of your star to a Command Strip or other hanger and hang it on the wall! Whenever you see it, consider the magic of making wishes for stars!

Chapter 4: DIY Leather & Faux Leather Projects

Leather is one of the uncommon fabrics for their Cricut that people get really enthusiastic about cutting. We can't tell you how many times someone has told us: we didn't know the Cricut could cut leather! The Cricut does not only cut leather, but it can cut fake leather as well!

Cricut develops a wide variety of fake leather in various colors and patterns. We'll be using real leather as well as fake leather and faux suede in this segment. In either of these designs, feel free to substitute genuine leather for fake leather or faux leather for genuine leather!

4.1 DIY Leather Headphones Keeper

With leather (or fake leather), you can create so many fun items! Bracelets, earrings, keychains, wallets, journals, and much more!

Your headphones are kept knot-free by the little cord-keepers, and they are super adorable too! Offer them as presents (they make a perfect gift for a hard-to-buy-for teen), create one for yourselves, and hold the hassle of twisted cords at bay!

Machine: Cricut Explorer or Cricut Maker

Items:

- Brayer tool

- Snaps with an extra-long post if using leather, or regular length for using faux leather

- Snap press

- Deep-point Blade

- Snap hole tool

- Headphones Keeper cut file

- Cricut leather or faux leather in your favorite color

- Strong Grip cutting mat

Directions:

Phase 1: log into the Cricut Modeling Room and upload a cut file for the Headphones Keeper.

Phase 2: after tapping on the design, then using either the arrow that resides in the lower right-hand corner of the design or the Sizing option in the upper toolbar, scales the design to 6.5 inches in length.

Phase 3: please press Make It. Set the sort of leather you're using for your cutting stuff. Through your Cricut, mount your deep-point blade. Place the polished side of the leather flat on your cutting mat. To drive the leather back onto the mat, use the brayer stone by using the arrow on the right-hand side of the Cricut to load your slicing mat into your Cricut. Look for the Cricut C to begin blinking once your mat is loaded, click the trigger, and your computer will start cutting.

Once your machine has done cutting, make sure that your template has sliced all the way through before using the arrow to unload the mat. To make the Cricut repeat the cut, click the Cricut C if it hasn't. When your computer completes cutting, and you are happy that all the way through your template is sliced, click the arrow again, and it will unload your mat.

Phase 4: peel off the cutting mat with your leather pattern. Three corners of the triangle fold in. To punch a hole wherever your snap heads, use your snap hole tool and then apply snaps to the headphone keeper with your snap click.

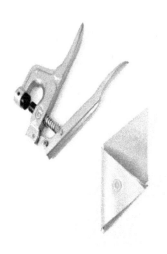

Hold inside the ear keeper with your headphones, and embrace tangle-free headphones!

4.2 Leather Heart Key Chain for Mom

The happiest and worst work in the whole world is a parent. If you're a parent, the fact is well known to you. We are making a Mom Keychain DIY Leather Core! Pop your deep point blade into your Cricut Maker or Cricut Explore. Let's get designing! This design is so fast and simple; this could possibly be completed in 5 minutes.

Machine: Cricut Explore or Cricut Maker

Items:

- E6000 glue

- Keyring

- Deep-point blade

- Fine-tip blade

- Something heavy like a stack of books

- Strong Grip cutting mat

- Brayer tool

- Black iron-on

- Regular grip cutting mat

- Mom Keychain cut file

- Cricut leather in your two favorite colors

- Weeding tools

- Iron-on protective sheet

- Easy Press or iron

Directions:

Phase 1: sign in to the Cricut Modeling Room and upload the Mom Keychain cut file.

Phase 2: by tapping on the design while using whether the arrow that resides in the bottom right of the design or the Sizing tool in the top toolbar, scale the design to 5 inches wide.

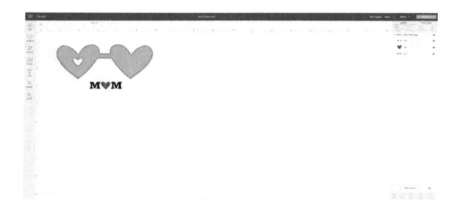

Phase 3: please press Make It. Parts of the heart are cut from leather. Set the sort of leather you're using for your cutting stuff. Through your Cricut, mount your deep-point blade. Lay down the clean side of the leather on the Good Grips cutting pad. To drive the leather back onto the mat, use the brayer stone using the arrow on the right-hand side of the Cricut to load your cutting mat into your Cricut. Look for the Cricut C to begin blinking once your mat is loaded, click the trigger, and your computer will start cutting.

When your computer has done cutting, make sure your template has sliced all the way through before using the arrow to offload the mat. To make the Cricut repeat the cut, click the Cricut C if it hasn't. When your device completes cutting, and you are happy that all the way through your template is sliced, click the arrow, and it will offload your mat.

The item "M M" is cut of black iron-on on a standard grip-slicing pad with the glossy black side down. Do not even overlook to duplicate the portrait on the left-hand side by using a mirror slider underneath the mat. Ensure you set the sort of iron-on you're using to set the cut environment.

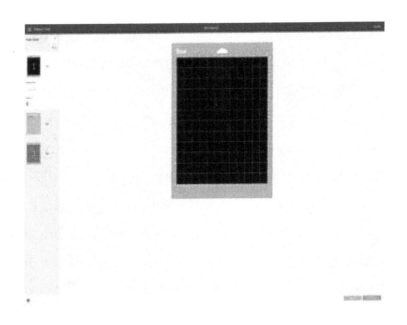

Phase 4: weed the iron-on, leaving the transparent plastic backing with only the 'M M.'

Phase 5: inside the big leather heart, pop the little leather heart. On top of the main piece of your keychain, put your iron-on. Lay the Cricut Protective Iron-On Layer over your leather and iron-on, and push with your iron or your Cricut Easy Press set at 280 °F for 30 seconds. The tiny leather core should be balanced between the two Ms. Check to ensure that the iron-on adheres to the leather and the transparent plastic cover is then slowly stripped away.

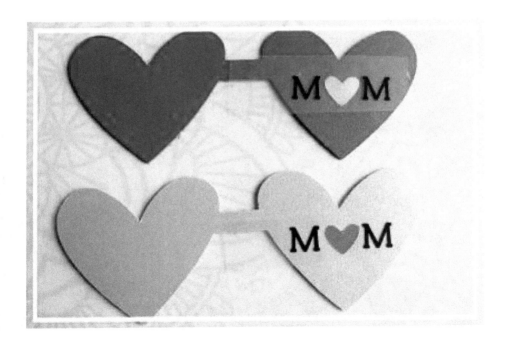

Phase 6: fold the heart in half and put the ring on the rectangular region that links the two hearts by slipping the keyring over it. Lay the leather with the side facing down with "mum" on it. Glue the two sides of the keychain together with your E6000 glue. Pinch the sides shut and rub out any glue that could leak out. Place the keychain for twenty-four hours under a stack of thick books so that the glue has time to recover.

Send this keychain to your mom to let her know she's still in your heart.

4.3 DIY Leather Teardrop Earrings

You'll love this project if you are making homemade presents for your friends! They're fun and bright, but they're also cheap to make! Eleven pairs of earrings can conveniently be made out of one sheet of leather and one HTV roll! For party favors, teacher gifts, bridesmaid gifts, and "just because" presents for relatives, these pretty earrings will be great! Play about with various sizes of earrings, different leather patterns, and different HTV finishes. These jewelers with faux leather can also be made to help your design dollars go even faster!

Machine: Cricut Explore or Cricut Maker Project

Items:

- Jewelry pliers

- Jump rings (2 rings for each pair of earrings)

- Earring hooks

- Strong Grip cutting mat

- Brayer tool

- HTV in your favorite color/finish (we used glitter iron-on)

- Deep-point blade

- Regular grip cutting mat

- Teardrop Earring cut file

- Cricut leather in your favorite color

- Fine-point blade

- The leather tool, needle, or safety pin

Directions:

Phase 1: sign in to the Cricut Design Space and insert the cut file for Teardrop Earrings.

Phase 2: size your earrings to the size you want them to be cut into. Press on the design to do it and use the arrow that occurs to size your earrings in the right-hand corner. They will cut four of the teardrops out of leather. Split out two of the smaller, iron-on teardrops.

Phase 3: please press Make It. Set the sort of leather you're using for your cutting stuff. Through your Cricut, load your deep-point blade. Lay down the clean side of the leather on your Strong Grip cutting mat. To drive the leather back onto the mat, use the brayer stone using the arrow on the right-hand side of the Cricut to insert your cutting mat into your Cricut. Wait for the Cricut C to begin blinking until your mat is mounted, click the trigger, and your device will start cutting. Offload your Cricut Leather Mat. Cut the HTV using a blade with a fine tip. Lay the HTV on a regular grip-cutting mat with the shiny-colored side facing down. Place the iron-on form you're using for your Cricut. On the left-hand side of the panel, mirror the layout using the mirror slider on the cutting mat.

When your device has done cutting, make sure your design has sliced all the way across before using the arrow to offload the mat. To make the Cricut replicate the cut, click the Cricut C if that hasn't. Once your device completes cutting, and you are happy that all the way through your layout is sliced, push the arrow again, and it will offload your mat.

Phase 4: weed the iron-on, cut the area around the outline of the earring, leaving the plastic backing with only the teardrops.

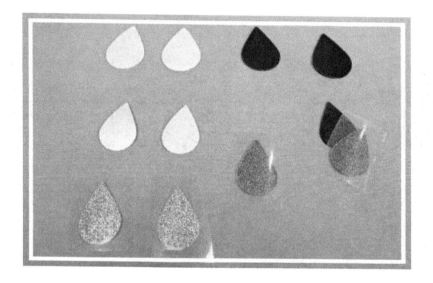

Phase 5: heat your iron or Easy Press. Lay the iron-on glitter on top of a piece of leather that is the same size. Click on the instructions for the iron-on form you're using. We pushed it for 20 seconds at 270 °F.

Phase 6: poke a hole at the top of each teardrop with a leather tool, needle, or paper clip. To thread a jump ring through the hole, you have punched in the fabric, use jewelry pliers and then tie the jump ring to your earring hook.

Phase 7: you made a stunning pair of earrings in leather! What kind of earrings are you allowed to make next? Dream of the different shapes you can make with leather and how you can decorate them. How do iron-on patterns look? With your Cricut Creator and a debossing tip, you might also "draw" on your leather.

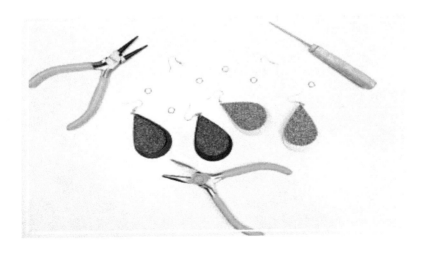

4.4 DIY Create a Journal Cover

In this venture, we're using fake leather with wood grain, but you might use standard leather as well. We are going to add an HTV decal to the front that says, "Create a Beautiful Life" to give this leather a beautiful, one-of-a-kind look. You might also keep the front of the cover blank, use a quotation of your own, and even insert a logo! Play about with various fake leather or leather colors and finishes to give this Journal an appearance that's also 100 % perfect as special as you are!

Machine: Cricut Explore or Cricut Maker Project

Items:

- Coordinating thread

- Easy Press or iron

- Easy Press Mat or a towel to protect your work surface

- Regular grip cutting mat

- Fine-point blade

- Sewing machine

- Journal Cover and Create a Beautiful Life cut files

- Two pieces of Cricut faux leather in your favorite color and finish (we used a wood grain faux leather)

- HTV in your favorite color

- Weeding tools

- Wonder clips or bulldog clips

Directions:

Phase 1: sign in, upload the Journal Cover, and Build a Gorgeous Life cut files to Cricut Design Space.

Phase 2: tap on and scale each journal item. You'll like to estimate the width of the Journal for the huge chunk, twice it, and attach 1 inch. You would want to weigh the height of your Journal and add 1 inch to it for the height. Adjust the height for the two small bits because they're the same height as the main cover piece of the book. We wanted to use one color from outside the Journal for our project and a second color for the inside flaps.

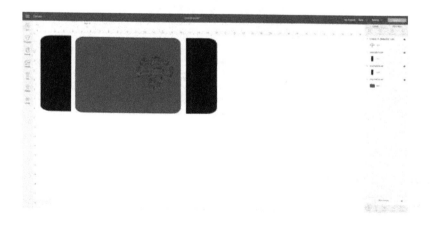

Phase 3: please press Make It. Set the sort of faux leather you're using for your cutting stuff. On your cutting mat, lie your imitation leather using the arrow on the right-hand side of the Cricut to bring your cutting mat into your Cricut. Wait for the Cricut C to begin blinking when your mat is mounted, click the button, and your machine will start to cut. If Cricut has stopped cutting, press the arrow button again to unload the mat.

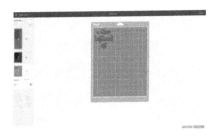

Cut the iron-on on the pad with the colored hand facing down. Use the mirror slider mostly on the cutting board on the left side of the screen to set the Cricut iron-on when cutting and mirror your pattern.

Phase 4: with the completed side facing down, place your long strip of faux leather on your worktop. With the polished side facing up, place the two smaller bits of faux leather on top of the large piece. On the right, line up one part, and on the left, the other piece. Clip into place.

Phase 5: use your sewing machine to stitch using a -inch seam allowance all the way across your Journal covering. Once you start stitching and again at the end, make sure to backstitch.

Phase 6: weed the iron-on, removing the area around the words, leaving the plastic backing with only the design. Don't forget to weed the letters inside as well (for example, inside the e, a, f, etc.).

Phase 7: heat the Simple Press or iron to the required temperatures for the iron-on you are using. Set your iron-on where you like it to be put on the cover of your book, using the guidelines for the sort of iron-on that you are using to click.

Phase 8: slip your Journal's front and back covers between the flaps of your journal cover.

Conclusion

So, that's the highway's limit. If all the ideas and techniques given in this guide have been learned, then cheers! In order to make sure that you get better at the earliest, you can hold on with this, before you can deal with things.

However, you must press high after learning the stuff. Keep this masterpiece close to you for purposes of reference.